How to Improve Your Spelling and Vocabulary

BY JESSICA DAVIDSON

A Language Skills Concise Guide
FRANKLIN WATTS
New York | London | Toronto | Sydney | 1980

Library of Congress Cataloging in Publication Data

Davidson, Jessica.
How to improve your spelling and vocabulary.

(A Language skills concise guide)
Includes index.
SUMMARY: Outlines techniques to help readers
improve spelling and vocabulary.
1. English language—Orthography and spelling—
Juvenile literature. 2. Vocabulary—Juvenile
literature. [1. English language—Spelling.
2. Vocabulary] I. Title. II. Series: Language
skills concise guide.
PE1145.2.D3   428.1   80–13797
ISBN 0–531–04133–6

Contents

Chapter 1.
Stop and Look

There's a question coming up. To answer it, don't write anything down. Don't spell out loud. And don't try to count in your head. Here's the question: How many vowels does your full name contain, how many consonants, and how many syllables?

If you don't know, it's not at all surprising. Most people don't, unless they happen to have very short names. Why should they? They've never had any reason to look at their names in that way. But if you do begin to observe words in that way, spelling will become a lot easier. That's because correct spelling is largely a matter of seeing. The good, natural spellers—the ones who don't seem to have to memorize anything—examine a word to see if it "looks right." You can't know that unless you've really observed the word in print and seen what it's supposed to look like.

For example, you should have no trouble in recognizing these misspelled words and deciding how they're supposed to be pronounced:

jiant   kat   tchild

Yet surely these words don't look right to you.

Don't misunderstand. No one is suggesting that, as you read a book, you should stop to analyze each word, break it down into syllables, and count the vowels and consonants. If you did, you'd get very little reading done and you'd understand even less of what you had read. But when you decide you want to learn how to spell a particular word, it is helpful to look at the word closely, to see how it is put together.

English spelling is not, for the most part, logical. If you were inventing a language, you could certainly invent one with a more reasonable spelling. You could set up rules to be followed without weird exceptions. But nobody "invented" English. The language developed and grew over many centuries, picking up words from other languages as it went along. The rules of spelling and pronunciation, the very alphabets of these languages, differed from one another. That is how English became a sort of patchwork quilt.

When a word is absorbed from another language, it is sometimes taken with its original spelling but is pronounced to follow English rules. An example is *Paris.* We have no trouble spelling *Paris* since it's pronounced as it's spelled in English. But the French say the city is named "pa-ree'," because that's the way it's pronounced in French.

Sometimes when we borrow a word from a foreign language we retain both the foreign spelling and the foreign pronunciation. An example of this is *pizza,* where the z's are certainly not pronounced as they are in *jazz.* It is this type of borrowing that causes great confusion in spelling. Why should *chauffeur* be spelled with a *ch* when the sound is "sh"? Because the word is French, and, in French, *ch* always sounds like "sh." Why should *cello* be spelled with just a *c* when the sound is "ch"? Because *c* (when followed with *e* or *i*) is always pronounced "ch" in Italian. In *scheme,* the spelling is Greek. In *schuss,* the spelling is German.

By understanding derivations from other languages, you can make sense of some of the peculiarities of English spelling. If you have found these peculiarities very frustrating, bear in mind that these same peculiarities make reading English difficult. In spite of these difficulties, you have certainly learned how to read. You might not be able to explain how you know that the following words don't rhyme, but you recognize readily that they don't:

cough   though   through   rough   bough

Suppose you encountered a similar word that was unfamiliar to you—slough, perhaps. You'd probably feel you'd have to look it up to know which of the five words above it rhymed with. Or would you just guess?

Looking it up is a skill in itself. Perhaps you haven't had much experience using a dictionary to discover how a word is pronounced. If so, now is the time to acquire that experience. A college dictionary is the most useful kind. An unabridged dictionary is too heavy for daily use. It contains much more information than you're likely to need. That extra material may even get in the way of what you do want to find out. So use a college dictionary if you can.

Somewhere in your dictionary—probably at the bottom of every other page—there is a key to the pronunciation of all vowel sounds and some consonant sounds. Notice particularly the very precise distinctions made between the sounds of "oo" in *loot* and *foot* and the sounds of "you" in *few* and *furious.*

Now look up *slough.* You will find that it has several different pronunciations and meanings.

The dictionary also tells us on which syllable of a word to place the stress. Dictionaries vary as to where they put the stress mark ('). Sometimes it's just *before* the accented syllable, sometimes it's just *after.* Check which way your dictionary works by looking up words you already know. You might, for example, look up the word *object,* which is both a noun and a verb, depending on how it's pronounced. Does your dictionary show the noun as ob' ject and the verb as ob ject'? Or does it show 'ob ject and ob 'ject? Once you understand the method your dictionary uses, you can easily find the stressed syllable in any unfamiliar word.

It's important to be able to use a dictionary for pronunciation. Otherwise, your reading vocabulary is likely to outstrip your speaking and listening vocabulary by far. You won't be able to use in conversation the words you know. You won't be able to recognize them when others use them. (Would you have recognized *slough* in any of its pronunciations?)

Try the following as a pretest: Guess whether the accented syllable rhymes with the word in column A, column B, or column C. On a separate sheet of paper, note down your answers. Do not use a dictionary at this point, but after you have finished, check your answers with those in the answer key of this book.

	Example:	A	B	C
1.	resuscitate	clue	bus	lie
	Answer: B			
2.	incompatible	fat	say	from
3.	indigent	fig	sty	bin
4.	echelon	stretch	flesh	neck
5.	reticent	see	mice	bet
6.	recidivist	bid	wide	hive
7.	extrapolate	flap	sex	hole
8.	fortuitous	fruit	who	high

Perhaps you knew some of these eight words before. If so, you'll have no trouble fitting them into the following sentences, one to a blank. If not, just guess where the words belong. Write down your answers on a separate sheet of paper and check them with those in the answer key.

A. I can't understand how those two can be friends, since they have nothing in common and seem wholly _____.
B. Some criminals are reformed by serving prison sentences; not everyone is a _____.
C. They assumed she was poor because of her ragged attire. But in fact she had a huge bank account and was far from _____.
D. Do you know how to _____ a drowning person?
E. Only those in the highest _____ of the government wield real power.
F. Since a baby grows several inches a year, can you imagine what height the baby would attain if you were to _____ that pattern throughout its life?

G. She is basically a very private person, _____ to speak before a large crowd.

H. I did not expect to see my teacher at the supermarket; the meeting was purely _____.

Now use your dictionary to check the full pronunciation (not just stressed syllables) and the full meaning of each word. Say the words to yourself several times as you look at them. Do not spell them out. After you've read them aloud a few times, see if you can write them with correct spelling, from memory.

This is not a spelling test. You may never need to write these particular eight words, and unless you do, their spelling won't be important to you. It is a test of how carefully you look at a new word when you meet one. If you didn't do too well, don't worry. Careful looking takes practice.

Which of these groups of letters is easier to memorize in correct order:

CWPOQTB or CHATWORK?

Obviously CHATWORK is, for the simple reason that you can pronounce it. It doesn't matter that it isn't a real word. The point is that it makes sense to learn how to pronounce a new word as a way of learning to spell it. Orthoepy and orthography have much in common.

Do you know what the last sentence says? Can you read it aloud?

Chapter 2.
Stop and Listen

Lots of words can be spelled correctly if you know how they sound. Saying words aloud to yourself can be helpful provided, of course, that you say them right.

Each of the words below has a blank space. Can you fill in the blank four times, using a different vowel each time, to make words that match the definitions? Write your answers on a separate sheet of paper.

l_g
1. a piece of firewood
2. a part of the body
3. to stay behind
4. to pull a heavy box

h_t
1. very warm
2. a cap
3. not a strike or a foul
4. a small house

b_t
1. baseball equipment
2. wager
3. used her teeth
4. He'd like to ——— he can't.

Many words are commonly misspelled because people mispronounce them or hear them mispronounced. Have you heard people say "injun" for *engine*? *Since* you want to make *sense,* you'd better be careful with how you pronounce your *i*'s and *e*'s. Your spelling will improve.

Sometimes vowels are slurred over or left out entirely, as in these faulty pronunciations:

> charcter   horble   terble   sposed
> jewlry   accidently   famly

How are these really spelled and how should they be pronounced?

Sometimes vowels are added where they don't belong. What vowels are wrongly added here?

> athaletic   monsterous   disasterous   mischievious

Consonants are often left out in careless speech and then, as a consequence, in spelling. Can you correct on a separate sheet of paper these common mistakes?

> strick   reconize   fith   lanlord
> advanage   perfeckly   comftable   foward
> quanity   lenth   libary   goverment

The sounds of long vowels are much easier to say and to hear than those of the short vowels. As a second grader, you were probably told that the long vowels say their names. So they do, but, of course, so do pairs of vowels pronounced together as a single sound. The pair *ai* in *pain* is an example. There is no way to hear the difference between the sounds of long *ā* in *pain* and *pane* because there is no difference. But you should hear the two syllables of *mayor* as different from the one syllable of *mare.*

There are thousands of words in English whose spelling is uncomplicated. In them, the long vowel sounds are spelled with a single letter. The consonant sounds are spelled with the "normal" letters ("f" is *f,* not *ph*). Even if you've never heard some of the words on the list that follows and have no idea what they mean, you will have an excellent chance of spelling them correctly after you've heard them pronounced.

Get a pencil and paper ready and ask someone to read the list to you. The stressed syllable is the one with the stress mark (') at the end: re cite'. All the vowels are short—as in *cat, bet, bit, hot,* and *cut*—unless they are marked with a bar, as in hāte, hēre, hīre, mōre, and pūre. If any other pronunciation aids are needed, they are given in parentheses following the word. These aids are only for the person who will read aloud to you. All you have to keep in mind are these few simple guides:

Most words ending in the sound "us" are spelled with *ous.*
Most nouns ending in the sound "shun" are spelled with *tion.*
Most words ending in the sound "ee-un" are spelled *ian.*
Almost no words end in *v.* Always add an *e* after the *v,*
    whether the vowel sound is long, as in *dive* and *save* or
    short, as in *give* and *have.*
The ending *ary* is much more common than *ery.*
And for this list, don't do anything complicated. For example,
    don't write *ph* for the sound of "f" and don't double the
    consonants unnecessarily.

Are you ready? Here's the list:

1. de cap' i tā ted
2. in ten' tion al
3. trans mog' ri fy
4. kin es thet' ic
5. ex tra sen' so ry (*sory* as in yes *siree*!)
6. prē var' i cate
7. com pre hen' sive
8. per pen dic ū lar' i ty (*lari* as in *Larry*)
9. ex ec' ū tive
10. in cred' ū lous
11. dis pen sā' tion
12. car di o vas' cū lar (*dio* as in *radio*; *vas* rhymes with *class*)

13. vi   vi   sec′   tion   (*vivi* as in *vivid*)
14. im   ped′   i   ment
15. sec   re   tār′   i   at   (*tari* rhymes with *hairy*)
16. par′   a   gon   (*par* as in *Paris*)
17. ser   en   dip′   i   tous
18. fab′   ū   lous
19. in   di   vid′   ū   a   lize   (*di* as in *did*)
20. ad   ū   lā′   tion

At five points each, did you score at least 90 on this test? If you missed some, the chances are that those you missed had syllables with a sound like that of *uh* or the *er* of *her*. This is the sound that dictionaries indicate with the symbol ə or ər. The symbol ə is called the *schwa* (pronounced "shwah"). It is the trickiest one for spelling. Hearing the sound gives you no clue, as you can see by the following list of words in which the spelling of the schwa sound has been italicized:

America
element
per*i*l
*o*ppose
*u*pon

You cannot listen for the difference in sound between *effect* and *affect* (as verbs) or between the suffixes of divis*ible* and agree*able* and auth*or* and writ*er*, because there is none. Based on sound alone, there is neither rule nor logic to help you in spelling the sound of schwa. These are spellings that simply have to be memorized or figured out by rules based on something other than sound. In the next chapters you will see what rules there are.

Chapter 3.
"The Exception
Proves the Rule"

Back in the days of the British Empire, when Britain was the world's foremost naval power and English spelling was just what it is today, this riddle might reasonably have been asked:

What's the difference between the English navy and the English language?

Answer: The navy rules the waves and the language waives the rules.

There are some rules for English spelling, but every last one of them has some exceptions. The old maxim, "The exception proves the rule," doesn't mean what you might think it does. "Proves" in this sentence doesn't mean "establishes the truth of." It's the "proves" of "proving grounds," where cars are tested to see if they meet performance standards. Exceptions *test* rules, and just about every rule of English spelling fails the test. Still, it's useful to become aware of the rules because a great many words do follow them.

It is certainly of some help to realize that if you know how to spell *at* and *ate,* you also know how to spell such words as *fat* and *fate, rat* and *rate,* and so on. The pattern here is one of pronunciation, but it helps in spelling, too: A one-syllable word with a single vowel and a single consonant at the end has a short sound for the vowel; if you add a silent *e* at the end, the first vowel becomes a long vowel: *hat* changes to *hate, met* to *mete, pin* to *pine, not* to *note,* and *cur* to *cure.*

There are exceptions. *Give* and *live* don't rhyme with *hive,* and *done* and *gone* don't rhyme with *bone* as they should if a silent *e* at the end always lengthened the vowel sound. But it's a good rule. It works most of the time, and it comes in handy when you're trying to decide what to do when you add the suffixes *-ed, -er,* or *-ing* to words such as *strip* and *stripe.* Was the paint on the car *stripped* or *striped*? Which did you mean to write?

The phrase *dinner in the diner* or the command "Stop whining! You're winning!" may help you to remember the rule: A silent *e* (as in *whine*) is dropped before *-ed, -er,* and *-ing*; a single consonant is doubled before adding the suffixes.

You might want to practice this rule by filling in columns for a group of words in this way:

thin   thinned   thinning   thinner
fine   fined   fining   finer

Here are some words you can use:

star   stare   tap   tape   grip
gripe   spot   ice   grin   line   flap
time   ship   cure   close

This rule is one of the most useful ones, because it seems to have only two exceptions. The exceptions are words ending in *x* (since *x* is never doubled) and words ending in *c* (of which there are very few to which these suffixes can be added). The *x* words don't change: *fix, fixed, fixing,* and *fixer.* The *c* words put in a *k* to keep the hard sound of *c*: *picnic, picnicked, picnicking,* and *picnicker.* If it were spelled *picnicing,* you'd want to read it to rhyme with *slicing,* and if it were spelled *picniccing,* you'd try to pronounce the *cc* like the *cc* in *success.* That's why it's *picnicking.*

Does the rule work for words of more than one syllable? Well, partly. Words that end in a silent *e* behave just like one-syllable words. They drop the *e* before adding *-er, -ed,* and *-ing.* For example: *compute, computer*; *debate, debating*; *relate, related.* Words like *happen* and *begin,* whose final syllables have a short vowel and a single final consonant, are a bit trickier. You have to say the word to yourself and listen for where the stress falls. Hap' pen. Be gin'. Do you hear the difference between *offer* and *prefer*? The *er* is stressed in *prefer* but not in *offer.* In longer words it is sometimes harder to tell whether the final syllable is stressed or not, but if you listen carefully you can hear the difference between *handicap* (stressed) and *parallel* (not stressed).

Write the following words on a separate sheet of paper, one word to a line, and, if the final syllable is stressed, underline it:

repel   level   refer   travel   listen
frighten   compel   benefit   transmit   kidnap
admit   gallop   discover   diagram   consider
regret   occur   corral   excel   label

The words with underlined final syllables will double the consonant when they add *-ed* or *-ing.* The others will not. Complete your list to look like this:

offer   offered   offering
prefer   preferred   preferring

CAUTION: While you will never go wrong in using this rule, be careful about correcting other people's spelling. In Britain, words ending in *l* and some other words such as *program, benefit,* and *worship* double the final consonant even though the last syllable is not stressed. *Travelled, signalled,* and *benefitted,* are the usual spellings in Britain and are acceptable in the United States as alternate spellings. So, follow the rule yourself; it's reliable. But don't take bets that someone who doesn't follow the rule has made a mistake.

After all this, you must be ready for a nice simple rule. Here is one: Just about every other kind of word there is doesn't change at all when *-ed, -er,* and *-ing* are added. This is true even when the result looks as peculiar as these:

ski	skied	skiing	
radio	radioed	radioing	
canoe	canoed	canoeing	skier

Are there exceptions? Of course. These are discussed, however, in the next chapter under the heading "Verb Endings."

By now you should be an expert on the question of what happens when *-ed, -er,* and *-ing* are added to words. Test yourself. In each of the following, one word—and one word only—is spelled incorrectly. Can you find what word that is?

    1.   After I dieted for two months, I found that I had slimed down considerably.

    2.   I was hoping to catch the rabbit, but it hoped away too quickly.

    3.   When I inquired about traveling by plane, the agent refered me to the main office.

    4.   I noted that the rope had been knoted rather carelessly and that it was raveling.

    5.   Why aren't you in school? Were you expeled? Of course not. Classes were canceled for today.

What happens when other suffixes like *-ence, -ance, -ent, -ant, -able,* and *-ible* are added to words ending in a single consonant? Do you double the consonant or don't you? Here you have to ask yourself how the word *with its suffix* is pronounced. For instance, take the word *refer.* It doubles the *r* when *-ed* is added because the stress remains on the *-er* syllable. But when *-ence* is added and the word becomes *reference,* the stress is on *ref.* So you don't double the *r* for the word *reference.*

    Which of these spellings are correct: *preference, preferable, deterrent?*

Chapter 4.
The Weird Science
of IE and EI
and Other Menaces

Let's get something straight right away. There's no point in memorizing rules. The reason is not only that all the rules have exceptions, as they do. It's also because there is no time, when you need to spell a word, to stop and run through all the rules to see which one applies. That would be like trying to calculate the trajectory of the softball as it leaves the pitcher's hand before you took a swing at it.

Then why present rules? Because, to the extent that they do work—and *mostly* they do—they show that English spelling is not completely illogical. They give you a way of looking at words to see how they're put together. If you practice using the rules, they may become automatic for you. With this in mind, here are some rules to think about.

PLURALS

Most nouns simply add *-s.*

There is one unimportant exception and three important ones. These are the three:

1.   Some words would be impossible to pronounce if just an *-s* were added, *boxs* for example. You have to say it in two syllables, and every syllable must have a vowel. So the rule is: Nouns ending in *s, x, ch,* or *sh* add *-es* to form a plural.

glasses   boxes   riches   dishes

2.   Nouns ending in *y*, where the letter just before the *y* is a consonant (or *qu*), change the *y* to *i* and add -*es*.

daisies   soliloquies

This is a rather strange rule, since the words that end in *i* to begin with just add an -*s*. Thus the plural of *ski* is *skis* while the plural of *sky* is *skies*!

Nouns ending in a vowel + *y* just add -*s* to form the plural. So *key* becomes *keys*, not *kies* and not *keies*, and *donkey* becomes *donkeys*, not *donkies*. But there's one word in this group that shows that, if enough people misspell a word for a long enough time, the misspelling becomes acceptable spelling. If you consult your dictionary, you'll find that the plural of *money* is either *moneys* (as it should be) or *monies* (as it shouldn't be). Blame somebody's careless great grandparents for that one.

3.   Words ending in *o* are somewhat unpredictable. If there's a vowel (including *y*) just before the *o*, add -*s* for the plural:

studios   tattoos   arroyos   vireos

If there's a consonant before the *o*, most nouns will also just add -*s* or, at worst, give you a choice of adding -*s* or -*es*:

bronchos   torsos   altos   zeros or zeroes

There are a few exceptions—words that must add -*es*, for example—but there's no logic to determine which ones they are. The most common of these are:

echoes   heroes   potatoes   tomatoes

In general, though, you're fairly safe just to add -*s*.

4.   This is the unimportant exception. It's unimportant because it affects very few words in the language. But, in another sense, it's enormously important because a great many people don't seem to know that it applies *only* to those few

(15)

words. The problem concerns apostrophes. Apostrophes are first taught in school as devices to show possession:

Sally's books are the books that belong to Sally.

Or, they replace a letter omitted in a contraction:

Do not becomes *don't.*

But, for some strange reason, people start putting apostrophes everywhere, as if they were sprinkling salt. They use *'s* to show plurals. Many sign painters seem never to outgrow this childish mistake. Well into adult life they paint signs such as "We serve breakfast's." DON'T! The only time an apostrophe is used to show a plural is with one-letter words, initial abbreviations, and numbers:

A's   IQ's   4's

NOWHERE ELSE.

There are some noun plurals that flout all the rules. You know most of these already. Words like *geese, mice, sheep,* and *children* must simply be learned without resorting to rules. There aren't a great many of them to plague you, and they're so unusual that you're unlikely to forget them.

Now let's see if you've absorbed the rules and exceptions given thus far. There are five misspelled plurals in the list below. Write them on your paper as they should be written:

vallies	horses	buses
abilities	courtesies	babies
gases	radioes	sandwichs
lady's	energies	canoes
pianos	enemies	sopranos
monkies	colleges	delays
alleys	GI's	foxes

VERB ENDINGS

Look carefully at the words below:

1	walk	walks	walked	walking
2	match	matches	matched	matching
3	dine	dines	dined	dining
4	sin	sins	sinned	sinning
5	agree	agrees	agreed	agreeing

The first thing to notice is that there are indeed five different patterns. Which one does not just add -s? Which three do not just add -ed? Which two do not just add -ing?

The rule here is easier to show by example than to state in so many words. Most verbs follow pattern 1. Verbs ending in x, sh, or ch follow pattern 2. All verbs ending in a consonant and silent e follow pattern 3. All verbs ending in a single consonant on an accented syllable double the consonant before -ed and -ing as in pattern 4. Words ending in ee or oe follow pattern 5. Everything—well, almost everything—follows one of the five patterns. The exceptions are words ending in y, ye, and ie. These follow no rules at all. Look and learn:

> say   says   said   saying

Pay and lay follow this pattern. But most others look like this:

> stay   stays   stayed   staying

Words ending in ie look like this:

lie	lies	lied	lying
tie	ties	tied	tying or tieing!
die	dies	died	dying (But for the verb "to die," meaning to cut with a tool called a die, it's dieing!)
defy	defies	defied	defying

All words of two or more syllables follow this pattern. Words ending in *ye* look like this:

dye   dyes   dyed   dyeing
eye   eyes   eyed   eyeing or eying

And then, of course, there are the far-out exceptions for verb endings:

slept   gave   thought   had taught

and a few others for which there are no possible patterns.

ADJECTIVE ENDINGS

1. The suffixes *-ible* and *-able* can't be distinguished by sound or by meaning. This is an area where you're going to have to memorize or be prepared to look the word up whenever you need to use it. There's a rule that works some of the time, but it's by no means reliable: If, when you remove the suffix, you have a verb that can stand by itself, either as it is or with an *e* on the end or a *y* for an *i,* the ending is likely to be *-able*:

agreeable   likeable or likable   variable

If it can't stand by itself, it's probably *-ible*:

possible   inaudible   horrible   indelible

But the rule has many exceptions to both of its parts. For example:

sensible   defensible   educable   probable   capable

2. *-al* is an adjective suffix, forming an adjective from a noun:

fictional   directional   sensational

-ical is also an adjective ending:

identical   practical   metrical   economical

None of the following are suffixes used to make adjectives from nouns:

-il   -el   -le   -icle   -ickle

So, if you've got an adjective formed from a noun, you can bet that it will end in *-al* or *-ical,* not *-il, -el, -le, -icle,* or *-ickle. Little, nickel,* and *fickle* are adjectives, but they are not exceptions to the rule because they were not formed by adding a suffix to a noun.

Just to be sure you have the rule in mind, on your paper form adjectives from the following words by adding *-al, -ical,* or *-able,* whichever is appropriate:

incident   front   politic   read   astronomy
verb   maniac   size   comic   nonsense
accept   norm   comfort   knowledge

-LY ADVERB ENDING

Have you ever made either of these mistakes?

realy   accidently

You shouldn't. The rule for adding *-ly* to adjectives to form adverbs is one of the most reliable. Ninety-nine times out of a hundred, just do it—add *-ly.* The exceptions are these:

1. You can't have three *l*'s in a row. Drop one: *fully,* not *fullly.*
2. For most words that end in *le,* drop the *e* and add *y: gently,* not *gentlely.*
3. Words ending in *y* are tricky. Usually we change the *y* to *i: daily, gaily, trickily.* But for a few one-syllable words we don't: *dryly, slyly* (and sometimes *gayly*).

(19)

And what was wrong with *accidently*? You must add the *-ly* to the adjective *accidental,* not to the noun *accident*: *accidentally.*

4. Finally, watch out for two important everyday exceptions:

whole wholly
true truly

Now test yourself by forming adverbs from these adjectives:

oral natural dull careful happy
possible speedy cool strange awful
sincere sneaky entire lone still

**"I before e
except after c
or when pronounced 'ay'
as in neighbor and weigh"**

It's an ancient rule and a fairly good one—but only fairly. It takes care of words like *receive* and *piece,* which are among the most frequently misspelled words in the language. It's a rule worth learning.

Exceptions? Naturally. These are the ones most frequently encountered where *i* doesn't come before *e* and there's neither a *c* nor an "ay" sound to justify the spelling:

seize counterfeit leisure foreign
weird either neither height
stein (of beer, or in names like *Einstein,*
which come from German
where the rules of spelling are different.)

The words in which *i* comes before *e* *after c* are limited to cases where the *i* and the *e* are pronounced in two separate syllables, as in *science,* or where the *i* gives a "sh" sound to the *c,* as in *conscience.* The only true exception may be *financier.*

Six words in the following list are spelled incorrectly. Can you find them?

siege   feild   thier   deceive   species
fancier   shield   freight   cheif   believe
freind   shriek   society   cieling   anceint

Chapter 5.
The Greeks Had a
Word for It and
So Did the Romans

There is a mispelled word in this paragraph. Can you discover it?

If you understand prefixes and suffixes, you'll be a better speller. Two Latin prefixes are involved in the words of the first paragraph: *mis-*, which means "wrong" or "wrongly"; and *dis-,* which means "separating" or "reversing." Thus,

dis cover—the reverse of cover
mis spell—spell badly

So how many *s*'s are there in misspelled?

What words result from adding these prefixes to the root words shown below? Write them correctly on your paper and define each in light of the prefix's meaning.

dis-	*mis-*
able	behave
qualify	spend
associate	state
prove	fortune
like	lead
connect	take
taste	step
satisfy	inform
orderly	adventure
arm	treat
similar	understand
appear	trust

Knowing Latin and Greek prefixes is often helpful not only in spelling but also in guessing the meaning of unfamiliar words. You don't have to study the Latin and Greek languages. You will be learning some Latin and Greek by working backwards from a group of familiar English words.

Are you familiar with *interscholastic* and *intramural* sports? Which one refers to contests between teams of different schools? So *inter-* must mean "between." As you know, a *mural* painting is a wall painting, and *intramural* translates to "inside the wall." Which of the two prefixes, *inter-* or *intro-* (the more common form of *intra-*), belongs with these endings, whose Latin meanings are explained?

-fere (carry)	-vene (come)
-spect (look)	-vert (turn)
-cede (go)	-duce (lead)
-cept (seize)	-sect (cut)

These Latin root words that have just been defined can be used with other prefixes. Take *-spect. Circumspect.* What's the meaning of *circum-?* Magellan was the first explorer to *circumnavigate* the globe. Where did he sail? What is the *circumference* of a circle? So what does a very *circumspect* person do before buying a car?

Retrospect. What's *retro-?* What does a *retrorocket* do for a spaceship? What is a *retroactive* law? So which way are you looking when you view something in *retrospect?*

Suspect. Sus- is a form of the prefix *sub-,* and that's familiar in words like *subway, submarine,* and *subnormal* temperatures. So if you *suspect* some funny business, where are you going to look?

Some prefixes are tricky because, like some words such as *tear* (rip) and *tear* (eye-water), they have two quite different meanings. The Latin prefix *in-* means "in" or "into." It also means "not." Can you separate the following words into two columns on your paper to show where they belong by meaning? (Hint: There are not necessarily ten of each.)

in- meaning not   *in-* meaning in or into

Here are the words:

inflexible	indecent	incumbent
indisposed	invade	innocent
income	intrepid	inspect
incorporate	inborn	include
infinite	incomparable	infused
incarcerate	indent	indivisible
innate	insignificant	

So far, the prefixes and roots have all been of Latin origin. A great many English words are derived from Latin, but English also has borrowed heavily from other sources. Sometimes it uses both Latin and Greek words for the same ideas. The Latin word for man is *homo,* as in the term *homo sapiens,* by which our species is known. From this root we have the English word *human.* The French have *homme* and the Spanish have *hombre.* The Greek word for man is *anthropos,* familiar in the word *anthropology,* the study of man. But then, surprisingly, English has both *hominoid* and *anthropoid,* which are almost identical in meaning.

As you can see from this example, the Latin and ancient Greek languages were not very much alike. That is why it should not startle you to learn that a given sound might function as two entirely different words in the two languages. When English words are derived from both, the result is often confusing. *Homo,* as discussed, is the Latin word for man. It is also the Greek word for "the same" or "similar." *Homophones* are words that sound alike. Does your school group students of similar ability? If so, you have *homogeneous* grouping.

From which language do we get the term *homogenized* milk? From which language do we get the word *homicide?*

And what must the ending *-cide* mean? What do you call something that kills insects? Something that kills pests? Then there's *suicide*. What must *sui-* mean?

Do you know the words *paternal* and *fraternal*? (*Fraternal* may be less familiar than *fraternity*.) If you do, you can be certain of the meaning of *patricide* and *fratricide*.

A very common Greek prefix is *tele-*. What does it mean? Consider what these have in common: *television, telescope, telephone, telephoto,* and *telegraph.* What did you decide?

Sympathy is a feeling with someone. *Apathy* is a lack of feeling; *antipathy* is a feeling against. What, then, is the literal meaning of *telepathy*?

If you enjoy taking words apart and putting them together, you might try to think of as many words as you can that have their source in a particular Latin or ancient Greek root. These are some root words that form the basis of a great many English words:

spect = look (Latin)
pend = hang (Latin)
graph = write (Greek)
port = carry (Latin)
tract = draw or drag (Latin)
cred = belief or trust (Latin)

Can you think of at least three English words that are derived from each of these?

Not all prefixes and suffixes are Latin or Greek. Some come into English from other languages. In many cases the meaning is obvious. For example, what is the meaning of *-ful* in these words?

handful   houseful   roomful

Is the meaning somewhat different (but equally recognizable) here?

fearful   powerful   masterful   peaceful   wishful

What suffix can you add to *power* and to *fear* to create words that mean the exact opposite of *powerful* and *fearful*? Can you write the words that mean without noise, incapable of speech, without hope, and without thought?

Some suffixes have no meaning in themselves but are ways of transforming a word from one part of speech to another. For example:

-ly changes an adjective to an adverb
happy   happily
-y changes a noun to an adjective
gloom   gloomy
-er changes a verb to a noun
think   thinker
-ment changes a verb or (rarely) an adjective
to a noun
entertain   entertainment
merry   merriment
-ness changes an adjective to a noun
sweet   sweetness

You'll notice that the spelling of the suffix does not change, but the spelling of the word to which it is added may alter. The rules you used for adding *-ed* and *-ing* work here as well: a final *e* is dropped before suffixes that begin with vowels: *taste* to *tasty*. A final *y* after a consonant changes to *i*: *happy* to *happily* and *happiness*.

Now test yourself. Change these nouns to adjectives:

wealth   health   room   trick

Change these verbs to nouns:

involve   develop   amaze
enjoy   govern   treat

Change these adjectives to nouns:

great   tender   lovely   silly

Chapter 6.
Beginning, Middle, or End—
DGEUJ the Judge

The most useful rules, the ones you're likely to remember, are those you figure out for yourself by observation. Consider the spelling of the words *jam, original, rage,* and *bridge.* When is the "j" sound spelled with a *j*? When with a *g*? When with a *dg*? Look at some examples and see if you can figure out a rule for what happens when the "j" sound is the last sound in a word:

wage siege oblige loge huge
badge ledge ridge dodge grudge

First obvious conclusion: None of the words ends in *j.* The second conclusion is harder, but if you haven't figured it out yet, ask yourself what the difference in sound is between *cadge* and *cage.* Can you make up a rule based on this?

There are exceptions, but not many. The most important one is *college,* because if your rule is the right one, it ought to be spelled *colledge* (like *ledge*) but it isn't. What rule has been broken? Later on, check your answer with the one in the answer key, but don't look yet because there's more to this rule. Can you add to your rule just a bit to account for these spellings?

large merge fringe gorge bulge

Now check your rule with the one in the answer key.

Using your rule, write on your paper the correct spelling for the words whose sounds are given below. Remember that the difference between *rat* and *rate* is shown this way: *răt răt*

crĭnj wāj barj knowlĕj hĕj hŏjpŏj
gouj stāj wĕj strānj sĭnj refūj

One big exception you need to know: Where *-age* is a suffix or the syllable isn't stressed, the word is pronounced to rhyme with *edge*:

manage marriage carriage
dosage postage village

The "j" sound at the beginning or middle of a word is a little harder to pin down, but there are some things to notice. Consider *gorge* and *George.* The *g* can't sound like "j" unless it has an *e* or an *i* right after it. (The exceptions to this are so very, very few that they qualify as collector's items. See Chapter 11.) So most "ja," "jo," and "ju" sounds are spelled just that way:

jar jolly major pajama just

For the "je" and "ji" sounds, either spelling may be used at the beginning of a word—there's no telling:

jeer gently jinx giant

But in the middle, it's far more likely to be *ge* or *gi*:

origin magic menagerie

Can you find some rules for the spelling of the sound "k" in the middle or at the end of a word? Look at some examples:

back   speck   trick   flock   stuck
trickle   pocket   sicken   comic   frantic
musical   maniac   symmetrical

All the vowels are short, so that can't be the distinction. Maybe it's a question of stress. Does it help to know that *sac* and *tic* are exceptions? Check in the answer key to be sure your rule is correct.

Now look at these:

break   stake   bleak   cook
hike   spoken   striker

What rule could you make up here? Again, check in the answer key.

Using your rule, say which of these are correctly spelled. Then, on a sheet of paper, rewrite correctly those that are misspelled:

chiken   basik   unlok   tragik   naked
streak   publik   traffik   dramatik
thiken   soket   nikel   plastik

How will you add to your rule to explain these?

walk   jerk   think   cork   murky   risk

For the sound of "k" at the beginning of a word, the rules are hard to state. But if you look up *k* in the dictionary and flip through the pages, you'll notice something: some *ka* words, but not very many; very few *ko* or *ku* words, but a lot of *ke* and *ki*. How about *kl* and *kr*? And how are most words beginning *ce* and *ci* pronounced?

How are your observational skills progressing? Can you come up with a rule for spelling the sound of "ch" in *church, beach,* and *ditch*? Here's a strong hint: The main exceptions to the rule are these:

rich   which   such   much
and the Russian composer Tchaikovsky

What's the rule?
    If you know, you can easily spot the five words that are misspelled here. If you don't know, check in the answer key before doing the exercise.

clutch   dich   porch   beech
scortch   witch   scrach   fetch
tchoose   reach   couch   startch

In what other way is the sound of "ch" spelled? How are the following words really spelled?

forchən (luck)   krēchər (person or animal)
məchu′ ər (adult)

There are altogether too many ways to spell the "sh" sound:

o*c*ean   di*sh*   confe*ss*ion
spe*ci*al   *sh*ip   exhibi*ti*on

And these aren't even counting those words that are straight from French, a language in which *ch* is always pronounced "sh":

crochet   chauffer   chef   chalet   chaise longue   machine

But the situation isn't quite as bad as it looks. Notice where the *sh* spelling occurs. Can you think of any word that begins with *ce, ci,* or *ti* that is pronounced with a beginning "sh" sound? I can't. I can't think of any words ending like that either. Certainly *ssi* won't work in either position. So, at the beginning or end of a word, "sh" is *sh* and none of the others. (There is nothing that can be said about *sure* and *sugar,* except that you know these words already, and they've probably never given you any trouble. So don't worry about them now.)

"Sh" in the middle of a word is more of a problem. You have to look at how the word was put together.

If the word now ends with a suffix, what was it before the suffix was added? The spelling of the root word doesn't change in important ways. Look:

vanished minus the -*ed* was vanish
confession minus the -*ion* was confess
official minus the -*ial* was office
partial minus the -*ial* was part

It's not always that simple to see what the root word was. Sometimes you can think of words related in meaning. For example, to spell *social,* think of *society.*

Some words you just have to learn:

essential   mission   fission
passion   position   Martian
and that entirely unlikely one—fashion

Do you want to try your luck with this rule? To find the correct spelling for the sound "sh" in these words, ask yourself what the word was before the suffix -*ion, -ous,* or -*ial* was added and keep the final consonant:

relāshun   distrăkshun   grāshus   vĭshus
collĕkshun   imprĕshun   exershun
integrāshun   spāshus   complēshun   fāshul

Chapter 7.
Is Spelling a Boar?

It's the easy, everyday words that are the real culprits. You can be forgiven for not knowing how to spell *desiccate* or *supersede,* but if you write *dosen't* for *doesn't,* you'll be regarded as illiterate. The prescription is obvious: Learn the easy words and learn them well.

This may turn out to be a rather dull chapter but a useful one. It will attempt to give you some ways to remember the correct spelling for the most frequent goofs.

It's means *it is,* as in "*It's* out of gas."

Its means *belonging to it,* as in
"That's why *its* motor won't run."

The apostrophe on a pronoun shows that something has been left out. In this case, it's the *i* in *is.*

He's = he is.   She's = she is.   It's = it is.

In the following, the *a* of *are* has been left out:

they're = they are   we're = we are

They're going to put *their* books over *there.* We've already looked at *they're.* The way to remember *there* is that it goes with *here* and *where.* The way to remember *their* is that it's neither of the above and it can't be spelled *thier* because then it would have to rhyme with *pier* or *flier*. And "*I* before *e* except after *c* or when pronounced 'ay' as in neighbor or weigh"—or *their*.

I do or I *do not*. I do or I *don't*. He does or he *doesn't* (does not). The apostrophe after a verb shows that something's been left out—here, the *o* in *not*.

Whose book is this and *who's* going to sign for it? There's no logic to *whose*. Remember it by thinking it goes with *those*. *Who's* is logical. The apostrophe shows that an *i* is left out. *Who's* = *who is.*

It's *your* book and *you're* going to sign for it. Think that *your* goes with *our*. *You're,* of course, means *you are.*

Compounds with *all* are a strange group:

It's *all right*; it's never *alright*—
there's no such word.

But we *already* knew that. And now we're
all ready to learn something new. Already
means "by now." *All ready* means
"entirely prepared," or "everyone prepared."

It's *altogether* (entirely) great.
Let's repeat it *all together* (everybody at once).

Some homophones present problems. You're surely past the "which witch is which" stage, but how about these?

I've often *passed* here in the *past*. Or, to put it
another way, *passed* is the *past* tense of pass.

That button's so *loose* that you're bound to *lose* it.

If you step on the *brake* too hard you'll *break* it.

Why would the burglar *steal* the *steel* pin
unless he thought it was silver?

Here are some troublemaking odds and ends:

etc., not *ect.* This is an abbreviation for two Latin words—
et cetera—which means "and others like it."

asterisk. Often mispronounced, and therefore often misspelled as *asterick.*

nickel. This has been misspelled *nickle* so often that the misspelling is now acceptable as a variant.

drowned, not *drownded.* It's the past tense of *drown.*

exercise, not *excercise.* Remember it by thinking of how you
exert yourself.

today, tonight, tomorrow. Today = to + day; tonight = to +
night; tomorrow = to + morrow (so it couldn't have two
m's).

Most words ending in the "er" sound end with the spelling
-er. Quite a few end in *-or.* Very, very few end in *-ar.* The
common ones in *-or* and *-ar* should be memorized because
it's too tedious to keep looking them up:

> liar   grammar   calendar   peculiar
> similar   author   governor   neighbor
> professor   actor   operator   collector
> conductor   supervisor   familiar   janitor
> elevator   motor   vapor   behavior
> orator   doctor   senator   minor   major

If you're stuck without a dictionary, take a chance on *-er*; It's
by far the most common.

Some of the exceptions can be remembered by recalling
how they're pronounced when suffixes are added. When you
say these words aloud to yourself, you'll realize that they
can't be spelled *-er*: minority, majority, senatorial, oratory,
grammarian, peculiarity, similarity, authority, and familiarity.

Most words ending in *-ian* are pronounced with two
syllables at the end, as in *Indian.* So you know that *again*
and *captain* don't end in *-ian.*

Here is a suggestion. It may turn out to be the most helpful one in this book. Make a list of the common words you
misspell most often. They may be an entirely different group

from the ones discussed here. Set up your list in two columns. In the first column, write the word the way you usually do—wrong. In the second column, write it correctly. If it's a word like *you're,* put it in a short sentence. Look at your list every now and then until the second column looks right to you and the first looks foolish. Any time you're bored and inclined to doodle, practice writing the words correctly with your left hand (if you're right-handed). It takes a lot more thought and effort to write with the hand you don't usually use.

Chapter 8.
Ghoti Spells Fish

How does *ghoti* spell *fish*? That's easy:

> Take the *gh* from the word *laugh*.
> Take the *o* from the word *women*.
> Take the *ti* from the word *nation*.

Then you have the sound of f-i-s-h.

Try some more of these:

> *tuese*—what might that spell?
> Take the *tue* from *virtue*.
> Take the *se* from *rise*.

Did you *choose* correctly?

> *choiet*—any guesses?

> Take the *choi* from *choir* and then be silent.

What nonsense spelling can you make from the *mn* of *autumn,* the *et* of *crochet,* and the *olo* of *colonel*?
   Here are some other sounds you can try to make combinations from:

> *eu* from *Europe*   *uy* from *buy*
> *pn* from *pneumonia*   *tw* from *two*

ph from *telephone*	*gn* from *gnaw*
oe from *shoe*	*ci* from *social*
bt from *debt*	*eo* from *people*
psy from psychology	*pt* from *receipt*
rh from *rhyme*	*ai* from *said*
isl from *island*	

Using some of these, how might you spell *shine*? Can you show how *twaign* spells *ten* and how *boepteo* spells *booty*? What other crazy spellings can you concoct? Try them out on your friends and see if they can solve them.

What's the point of all this? Somebody once said, "How can a dictionary help me to find out how to spell a word since I can't look the word up unless I know how to spell it?" That's what this nonsense is good for. You hear someone say what sounds like "you fum izm" and you don't know how to spell it. What possible choices are there for the beginning sound of "you"?

you as in *you*

u as in *use*

ew as in *few*

eu as in *Europe*

How might you spell "fum" without using an *f*? Now can you find "you fum izm" in the dictionary? You'll know that you've found it if the word you've chosen refers to a phrase like "I'm going to wash up" when you really have something else in mind but don't want to actually say it. How is the word really spelled?

Can you find a word that sounds like "flem"? It means what you cough up when you have a sore throat.

Can you find a spelling for the word that sounds like "filter" and means a charm or drug?

Can you find the word that sounds like "roo mat izm"?

Here are some easier searches, with definitions of the words you're looking for:

ē mā′ she ate	to grow very thin
or ī′	twisted
spay shul	relating to space
spay shuss	roomy

Here's the most unlikely spelling of all. It sounds like "nice" and it's a rock. Can you find it?

Because of the great variety of ways of writing the same sound, there are some very unlikely looking rhyme groups. On a piece of paper, write down words that rhyme with each of the following. Note that each answer has a different spelling for the rhyme sound. The definitions of the missing words will help you.

To rhyme with *scourge*
(1) To persuade, to push
(2) Join, as two lanes of traffic
(3) A funeral song

To rhyme with *hurt*
(4) Soil
(5) Awake

To rhyme with *got*
(6) Which thing?
(7) Boat

To rhyme with *seek*
(8) Old valuable
(9) Not strong
(10) Arab chief

To rhyme with *force*
(11) Steed
(12) Naturally
(13) Origin
(14) Rough

To rhyme with *deuce*
(15) Not tight
(16) Alibi

(17) Fluid
(18) Temporary peace
(19) Frozen dessert

To rhyme with *beard*
(20) Was afraid
(21) Peculiar
(22) Showed derision with a smile or laugh
(23) Layered
(24) Stuck to

To rhyme with *nurse*
(25) Practice, as for a play
(26) Poetry
(27) Inferior
(28) Force
(29) Swear

By contrast, there are some pairs or groups of words in English that look as if they ought to rhyme but don't. And this brings us to homophones, words that sound alike but have different meanings. In the sentences below, can you, on a sheet of paper, replace the italicized words with their properly spelled homophones, to make some sense out of the sentences?

1. Have you ever *scene* a more beautiful *flour* garden?
2. The coffin was placed on a *beer.*
3. What is it like to be *air* to the *thrown*?
4. She has to watch her *wait,* but she'll *waist* away on that diet.
5. There was a *miner* problem concerning the passenger list on that *plain.*
6. Look at that *heard* of rams and *yews.*
7. Shakespeare lived during the *rain* of Queen Elizabeth.
8. *They're* children can fly for half *fair.*
9. I can't *right* in any language *accept* English.
10. Do you *no* the *hole* poem by heart?
11. He *through* them down the *seller stares.*

You might possibly have had some trouble—though it's doubtful—in replacing the italicized words in the eleven sentences above, but you certainly didn't have any trouble reading the sentences aloud and knowing the sounds of the words. But suppose the words were unfamiliar. If you'd never seen the word *choir*, how would you know what its homophone was?

Pretend for the moment that you're a foreigner learning English. Use your dictionary to find out how to pronounce *choir*, *quire*, and *choice*.

Chapter 9.
When Is
Best Worst?

When is best worst? When it's a verb. Your dictionary will show these definitions:

> best (vt)   to get the better of; outdo
> worst (vt)   to get the better of; defeat

So he *bested* them in a battle or he *worsted* them but, in any case, he won.

If someone called you a *flibbertigibbet,* a *quisling,* or a *garrulous gossoon,* you'd probably look the word up to discover whether or not the *epithet* was *pejorative.* Was it?

There's no problem about words like *quisling* and *pejorative.* If you don't know them, you don't know them and that's that. Either you couldn't care less, and you forget all about them, or you are sufficiently concerned to look them up in the dictionary and settle the question. Either way, you're not fooled. The words that fool you are the simple words, the ones you think you know and the words that sound like other words you know. The simple words often have a variety of meanings. You may latch onto one that's wholly inappropriate. "They spread their tablecloth on the river bank and opened their picnic basket" may not conjure up for you a picture of people munching on egg salad sandwiches near a vault. But if the only meaning you knew for *bank* was "a place to keep money," you would certainly find the sentence confusing.

There follows a list of sixteen words. Some of them you may know. Others you might think you could safely guess at. Each word has a definition beside it. Nine of the definitions are correct, though these are not necessarily the only possible correct definitions. *Bank,* for example, could be defined as "rely," for that is what it means in the sentence, "You can *bank* on that authority." The other seven definitions are simply wrong in any context. See if you can decide which are the wrong definitions. Just guess. Don't look anything up. List on your paper those you think are incorrect.

nice—precise	inflammatory—causing a riot
wit—common sense	flatulent—level
infamous—not well known	friable—suitable for cooking
entertain—consider	indifferent—similar
correspond—match	disinterested—impartial
noisome—loud	aseptic—clean
inflammable—flammable	apian—monkey-like
mean—average	fulsome—generous

Do you have a list of seven?

The correct definitions of the seven words wrongly defined above are these:

smelly   blown up   disgraceful   sickeningly insincere
crumbly   relating to bees   unconcerned

Can you match these definitions to the seven words you've listed?

Now here are all sixteen words used correctly in context. Check your definitions to see if they match.

Aseptic and antiseptic *correspond* closely in meaning. There is a *nice* distinction between them.

The defendant, who had a reputation for *infamous* behavior, was accused of making *inflammatory* speeches.

The judge *entertained* a motion to dismiss the charge.

A *disinterested* study showed that the *mean* income of doctors was higher than that of engineers.

The alleyway was cluttered with *noisome* garbage and *inflammable* trash. No one could remain *indifferent.*

The politician's speech was full of empty promises, *fulsome* language, and *flatulent* rhetoric.

Handle that porcelain carefully. It's *friable* and almost as delicate as *apian* wings.

If only you'd had the *wit* to read the directions before you started!

Now's the time to look up some words if you're not sure. But the point of this chapter is not to get you to learn the meaning of these particular sixteen words. Rather, it is to caution you to look up words you *think* you know if the meaning you're familiar with or the one you have guessed doesn't quite seem to make sense.

What sentence might a baseball fan write using these three words: *fly, batter, pitcher*? What sentence might a cook write using the same three words?

Sometimes confusion occurs between members of a pair of words that sound somewhat alike but are wholly different in meaning. Here is a list of fifteen such pairs. Can you place them correctly in the sentences numbered to match? Write your answers on a separate sheet of paper.

1. impute—impugn
2. ingenious—ingenuous
3. unanimous—anonymous
4. flout—flaunt
5. conscious—conscience
6. incredulous—incredible
7. indigent—indignant
8. principal—principle
9. adapt—adopt
10. eminent—imminent

11. allusions—illusions
12. compliment—complement
13. accept—except
14. fortunate—fortuitous
15. personal—personnel

1. He _____ed my reputation by _____ing the crime to me.
2. I would not have expected such a clever, _____ excuse from such a naive and _____ girl.
3. Although the author of the suggestion modestly remained _____, the idea met _____ acceptance.
4. She disobeys the law and likes to _____ the rules all the time and then has the audacity to _____ her disregard of authority.
5. Are you _____ of the fact that you have a _____, a lively sense of what is right and what is wrong?
6. He found the story _____ and, refusing to accept it, remained _____.
7. The old man who had been sleeping on the park bench was _____ at being awakened and assured the police officer that he was neither a vagrant nor _____, having a home of his own and money in the bank.
8. The social studies teacher explained that for him it was a matter of _____ to teach the mineral wealth and _____ products of each country under discussion.
9. Foreigners need not _____ our language as their own but would do well to _____ their behavior to conform to local customs.
10. The _____ physician examined the accident victim and said she feared his death was _____.
11. When the psychiatrist reported his findings did he mention or make any _____ to the hallucinations and _____ of the patient?
12. I'm not sure that my work deserves the _____ you paid it, but I must say that I find your praise the perfect _____ to a wonderful day.

13. The official would _____ no proof of age _____ a birth certificate.

14. Just my luck to run into the boss's son at the ball game when I was supposed to be home sick. It was an entirely _____ meeting and certainly not a _____ one.

15. The _____ manager asked some very _____ questions when she interviewed me for the job.

Chapter 10.
Hangman, Ghost, and
Other Spelling Games

BUILDING AND BEHEADING

This is a good game to play while waiting for a bus or when stuck in a traffic jam. No pencil or paper or other equipment is required. Here's a sample:

> You can sit on it, but if you cut off its head it will be on your head, and if you cut off its head again, you can breathe it.

We're looking for three words. What are they? Just to get you started, I'll tell you: *chair, hair,* and *air.*
Here's one that goes in the opposite direction:

> Start with a package of paper—500 sheets. Put a head on it and pour it into your coffee. If you don't like the result, put another head on it and yell!

What riddle could you make up to go with host–ghost? With laughter–slaughter? With ate–rate–crate? What other good pairs or triplets come to mind?

HANGMAN

Hangman is very well known. It's a game that's been around for years. Your grandmother probably knows how to play it.

In the unlikely event that you've never encountered it, here are the basic rules:

One player, the hangman, thinks of a word or phrase (not a proper name) and draws the correct number of dashes to represent the letters. The other player, or team of players, guesses one letter at a time. If the letter is in the word, the hangman writes in the letter above the proper dash or dashes, wherever and as often as it appears. If the letter occurs nowhere in the word, the hangman begins the hanging by drawing a gallows and the outline of the head for the first mistake. For later mistakes, the ears, eyes, mouth, nose, body, arms, and legs are added until the hanging is complete. Players try to fill in the spaces before this can happen.

Some words are much easier to guess than others.

$$\_\_ \quad A \quad \_\_ \quad A \quad \_\_ \quad A$$

If it's not *cabana*, what is this word almost sure to be?

The shorter the word and the fewer the vowels, the harder it is to guess. Double letters make it easier unless the letters are ones very unlikely to be chosen. CRYPT is very likely to hang someone. SCYTHE is almost as bad. BETTER, on the other hand, is very easy because, since *e* and *t* are the letters most frequently used in English, they are most likely to be chosen.

A skilled hangman player calls vowels first, beginning with *e,* and then switches to consonants as soon as there is one vowel filled in for every three blanks.

GHOST AND SUPERGHOST

This is another fine game for traffic jams or any tedious, time-wasting situation. No equipment is needed nor, for that matter, allowed. Any number can play, but three to five players make the best game.

Everyone takes a turn announcing a single letter that, with the existing sequence, will form some word. But the object is *not* to end the word, but rather to force someone else to end it. Three letter words don't count. After three letters, if the letter you say ends a word (whether it's the one you had in mind or not), you lose that round. You become the G of the ghost. Five words ending on you and you're out of the game as you become the H, the O, the S, and the T of the ghost—unless, of course, someone else loses first.

When it's your turn you must say a letter and you must have some word in mind that you can reveal if you're challenged. If you are challenged and cannot give a word, you get a letter of the ghost. If you're not challenged, you don't tell anyone what word you're thinking of. You can change your mind as often as you like.

A game among Mary, Joe, and Dana might go like this:

Mary: A

Joe: C

Dana: T (A word has ended, but it's only three letters, so there's no problem. Dana is thinking of ACTOR, which would end on Joe.)

Mary: I (Mary is thinking of ACTION, which would end on Dana.)

Joe: V (Joe is thinking of ACTIVE and expects Dana to lose this round.)

Dana: A (Dana has thought of a way out.)

Mary: I challenge you. (Mary has thought of ACTIVITY, but the A won't fit. She believes Dana is bluffing.)

Dana: The word is ACTIVATE. (It would have ended on Joe and he'd be the G of the ghost, but since Mary challenged, Mary is the loser. She's the G of the ghost.)

The game now starts its second round, beginning with Mary (because she lost the previous round). It continues until all players but one have become the G-H-O-S-T of the ghost. The remaining player wins.

Very superior spellers can play Superghost. In this game, each player has the option of adding a letter to either end of the sequence. Here is an example:

Mary: A

Joe: C

Dana: T

Mary: I

Joe: O

Dana: R in front. (Seeing no way to go on without ending the word ACTION, Dana thinks of FRACTION, which would end on Joe.)

Mary: N at the end. (This is now a safe play because RAC-TION isn't a word.)

Joe: E in front. (Joe cannot think of a word that doesn't end on him. His only hope is that someone will challenge him. His word is INTERACTION and he hopes that either Mary or Dana won't figure it out. Joe could have said S at the end so that FRACTIONS would end on Dana, but that didn't occur to him.)

SEQUENCES

People who are good at Superghost (or people who would like to become Superghost experts) will also enjoy sequence puzzles. Any number can play, no equipment needed. The idea is to think of a word that contains a particularly unusual sequence of letters and then to challenge others to find a word that contains the sequence. It does not have to be the word you were thinking of. For example, if, thinking of APARTMENT, you said, "My sequence is RTM," the answer DEPORTMENT would be acceptable.

If you can think up a sequence like OKK and challenge others to find it, they'll have to come up with your word, BOOKKEEPER, because there's no other choice. Proper names and sequences that occur only in foreign or obscure words are not allowed. HLR, for example, would be considered unfair because, as far as I know, it occurs only in the word KOHLRABI.

Sometimes you'll think you have a really difficult one like PLATYPUS, only to find that when you ask for TYP someone immediately says TYPE. That has to be accepted, of course.

Try these for starters. They're all quite ordinary words:

AGM   THL   MPL   IIN   GNE   THH

The answers given in the answer key of this book are only possible answers and not necessarily the ones you'll come up with. If your answer is in the dictionary and it's not capitalized, you've won.

The usual challenge is a three-letter sequence, but it can be longer if you like. Here are three of the toughest challenges, although all are common, everyday words and RSTU has at least two answers. Please don't give up for at least twenty-four hours. Then you can check the answer key of this book.

RSTU   ANW   ERGRO   and a bonus for science buffs: IOI

Chapter 11.
Puzzles, Tricks, and
Word Collections

WAS IT A CAR OR
A CAT I SAW?

A ridiculous question, wouldn't you say? Of course. But it's a special question, as you'll see if you read it backwards, paying no attention to the spacing. Sentences like that one are called palindromes. The most famous long ones are these:

Able was I ere I saw Elba.

(That's what Napoleon is supposed to have said when he was exiled from France to the island of Elba.)

Madam, I'm Adam.

(Adam's first speech to Eve, perhaps.)

A man, a plan, a canal—Panama!

Palindrome sentences are extremely difficult to invent, but two or three word phrases are not so hard to come by. See if you can guess how these blanks would be filled. Write your answer on a separate sheet of paper.

Everyone makes mistakes. Teachers goof and *pupils* —————
————.

All the food was excellent, but the menu especially *stressed*

_____ .

They called him Dennis the Menace because, quite often,
Dennis _____ .

There are also many individual words like *radar* that are palindromes in themselves. Here is a group for you to complete on a separate sheet of paper. Please do not write in the book.

lev__ __	sex__ __	deif__ __ __
sol__ __	ref__ __	rot__ __
civ__ __	red__ __ __	to__ __
	revi__ __ __	

Can you find others?

DESPERATION?
A ROPE ENDS IT

Or, you might say, I NEED A SPORT. What goes on here? Do you NOTE DESPAIR? Or NEAT PERIODS?

What goes on, of course, is the pastime of anagrams— using the letters of a word to make another word or several other words. One kind of anagram challenge is simply to discover in how many ways the letters of a word can be juggled to form other words or word groups. But "a rope ends it" is a much more clever anagram for *desperation* than "neat periods" because of the association of meaning. So it is more fun to try to find compatible pairs.

Using the definitions as hints, can you find appropriate anagrams for the following words or phrases? Write your answers on a separate sheet of paper.

1. DORMITORY—not too clean a place to live (two words)
2. ADMIRER—what he did with the woman he admired
3. ENRAGED—a perfect synonym
4. ONE HUG—and that's plenty
5. SEA TRIP—who went on it, flying a black flag

6. RECIPES—their directions must be exact
7. BOREDOM—a place where you might find it if you're not sleepy
8. TRIFLING—one of the ways to trifle
9. OUR MEN EARN IT—it's their payment, a synonym for fee
10. MADE SURE—what they did to make sure how long it was
11. A STEW, SIR?—the one who asked this of the customer
12. STIPEND—what to do with a stipend (two words)
13. OUR PET, SAM—where he was caught because he loves cheese

WORD LADDERS

Here's another great game to be played alone. The idea is to go from one word to another, one step at a time. One letter is changed each time. The order stays the same and at each step you have a real word. Here is a ten-step ladder from RICH to POOR. Each letter change is shown in boldface type:

RICH

1.	RICE	6.	LOCK
2.	RACE	7.	LOOK
3.	PACE	8.	BOOK
4.	PACK	9.	BOOR
5.	LACK	10.	POOR

You could have a shorter ladder by going from RACE (2) to LACE and then on to LACK (5). Perhaps you can find an even shorter ladder.

How short a ladder can you construct
from HEAT to COLD (or from HOT to ICY)
from SICK to WELL
from GOOD to BEST
from HOUSE to CLASS
from LOSE to FIND?

Each can be done in ten steps or less, in some cases a lot less. Try going from ROOM to ROOM through the HALL by different paths (each less than ten steps).

MNEMOSYNE REMEMBERS

Mnemosyne was the Greek goddess of memory. Her name and the word *mnemonics*—a device to improve the memory—are the only words in the English language that begin *mn*. Mnemonic tricks are fun to invent. If you can create some like the following for the words you have trouble spelling, the gimmicks may prove useful:

> *Too* has too many *o*'s.
> *Am I able* to be *amiable*?
> Who needs a *fiend* for a *friend*?
> A *novice* has *no vice*.
> An *island is land*.

Here are some examples others have thought up for their spelling demons:

> attendance—*At ten, dance*!
> separate—What *a rat* of a word to spell!
> significant—How can I *sign if I can't* write?
> parallels—It's *all els*.

The gimmick doesn't have to make sense. Nonsense gimmicks like these may work for you.

> embarrass: ar! ra!—a backward cheer
> accommodate: si, si, mm! good!
> nickel: a buffalo nickel is a nick elk
> accept: I will accept a C
> except: everyone except me—ex my name out

And, if you can't think of any gimmick like these for your particular spelling problems, you can always sing the tricky part. Singing commercials stick in your mind and so will spelling songs. They're fine mnemonics.

WORD COLLECTIONS

People collect all kinds of things—stamps, matchbooks, coins, beer cans. Most collections take up space and have to be mounted, dusted, and generally cared for. But you can collect words. They're no trouble at all to care for, and they can improve your word skills tremendously.

Here are some examples of the kinds of word collections you can make. There are certainly many other possible kinds.

1. Words that use all the vowels:

dialogue

(*abstemious* and *facetious* are even better
because they use all the vowels in proper order)

2. Words with double letters—one for every letter of the alphabet, if possible. Here are a few of the more difficult ones:

bazaar flivver glowworm

3. Words in which *g* is pronounced "j" or *c* is pronounced "s" before *a, o,* or *u.* These are extremely rare.

margarine facade

4. Words that are homonyms with opposite meanings:

cleave means "to stick" and "to break apart"
sanguine means "bloody" and "hopeful"

5. Words that look like opposites but have the same meaning:

ravel and *unravel*
solvent and *dissolvent*
flammable and *inflammable*

6. Words that break up amusingly into two or more other words, without altering the sequence:

manslaughter = man's laughter
capsize = cap size

7. Word pairs where the pronunciations of two successive letters are wildly different:

as*l*eep and is*l*and
di*sh*es and di*sh*onest
fri*ng*ed and ri*ng*ed
tele*ph*one and cho*ph*ouse
no*th*ing and po*th*older

You might want to collect words with the greatest proportion of consonants and the greatest proportion of vowels. My best so far are seven letters out of eight for the consonants and five out of seven letters for the vowels (see the answer key after trying to guess).

And for a final comment: Why is the pen mightier than the sword? Because it can turn the *sword* into *words.*

Answer Key

CHAPTER 1

p. 4
2A   3C   4B   5C   6A   7A   8B

pp. 4 to 5
A2   B6   C3   D1   E4   F7   G5   H8

p. 5
orthoepy = correct pronunciation
orthography = correct spelling

CHAPTER 2

p. 6

log	leg	lag	lug
hot	hat	hit	hut
bat	bet	bit	but

p. 7

character   horrible   terrible   supposed
jewelry   accidentally   family

p. 7
ath(a)letic   monst(e)rous   disast(e)rous   mischiev(i)ous

p. 7

strict   recognize   fifth   landlord
advantage   perfectly   comfortable   forward
quantity   length   library   government

CHAPTER 3

p. 11

star	starred	starring	_____
stare	stared	staring	starer
tap	tapped	tapping	tapper
tape	taped	taping	taper
grip	gripped	gripping	gripper
gripe	griped	griping	griper
spot	spotted	spotting	spotter
ice	iced	icing	icer
grin	grinned	grinning	grinner
line	lined	lining	liner
flap	flapped	flapping	flapper
time	timed	timing	timer
ship	shipped	shipping	shipper
cure	cured	curing	curer
close	closed	closing	closer

p. 12

repel	repelled	repelling
level	leveled	leveling
refer	referred	referring
travel	traveled	traveling
listen	listened	listening
frighten	frightened	frightening
compel	compelled	compelling
benefit	benefited	benefiting
transmit	transmitted	transmitting
kidnap	kidnaped	kidnaping
admit	admitted	admitting
gallop	galloped	galloping
discover	discovered	discovering
diagram	diagramed	diagraming
consider	considered	considering
regret	regretted	regretting
occur	occurred	occurring
corral	corralled	corralling

ex*cel*   excelled   excelling
label   labeled   labeling

p. 13
1. slimmed 2. hopped 3. referred
4. knotted 5. expelled
p. 13
Preference, preferable, and deterrent are all spelled correctly.

CHAPTER 4

p. 16
valleys ladies monkeys radios sandwiches

p. 19
incidental frontal political readable astronomical
verbal maniacal sizable or sizeable comical nonsensical
acceptable normal comfortable knowledgeable

p. 20
orally naturally dully carefully happily
possibly speedily coolly strangely awfully
sincerely sneakily entirely lonely stilly

p. 21
field their chief friend ceiling ancient

CHAPTER 5

p. 23
interfere   intervene
introspect   introvert
intercede   introduce
intercept   intersect

p. 24
in = *not*   *in* = *in or into*
inflexible   infused
indecent   inborn

indisposed	incarcerate
incomparable	income
indivisible	indent
infinite	incorporate
innocent	incumbent
insignificant	innate
intrepid	invade
	inspect
	include

pp. 24 to 25
homogenized from Greek
homicide from Latin
-cide = killing

sui- = self
tele- = far

p. 25
These are examples; there are many more:

spect	*pend*	*graph*
spectacle	suspenders	graphite
inspect	suspense	biography
suspect	independent	telegraph
perspective	pendulum	autograph
prospect	appendix	geography

port	*tract*	*cred*
import	attract	credit
transport	extract	incredible
portage	tractor	credentials
portable	retraction	credo
report	contract	credulous

p. 25
-ful, of course, means "full of."
power*less* is opposite of power*ful*; fear*less* is opposite of
fear*ful*

p. 26
noiseless   speechless   hopeless   thoughtless
(60)

p. 26

wealthy	involvement	greatness
healthy	development	loveliness
roomy	amazement	silliness
tricky	enjoyment	tenderness
	government	
	treatment	

CHAPTER 6

p. 27

For words with long vowels or consonants just before the "j" sound, the spelling is *ge*; for those with short vowels, the spelling is *dge*. Where a consonant comes just before the "j" sound, the spelling is *ge*.

p. 28

cringe	wage	barge	knowledge	hedge	hodgepodge
gouge	stage	wedge	strange	singe	refuge

p. 29

After a short stressed vowel the "k" is spelled *ck*; short un-stressed vowels are followed by *c*.

p. 29

After consonants or long vowels, it's *k* alone.

p. 29

Streak and *naked* are correctly spelled. The others should be spelled:

chicken	basic	unlock	tragic
thicken	public	traffic	dramatic
	socket	nickel	plastic

p. 29

Where a consonant comes just before the "k" sound, the spelling is *k*.

p. 30

The sound of "ch" is always spelled *ch* at the beginning of a word, after long vowels and consonants. After short vowels it's *tch*.

p. 30
ditch   scorch   scratch   choose   starch

p. 30
fortune   creature   mature

p. 31
relation (relate)   distraction (distract)
gracious (grace)   vicious (vice)
collection (collect)   impression (impress)
exertion (exert)   integration (integrate)
spacious (space)   completion (complete)
facial (face)

CHAPTER 8

p. 36
quiet
mnetolo = mare
ciislpn = shine, for example
tw from *two* + *ai* from *said* + *gn* from *gnaw* = ten
b + *oe* from *shoe* + *pt* from *receipt* + *eo* from *people* = booty

p. 37
euphemism
phlegm
philter
rheumatism

p. 38
emaciate
awry
spatial
spacious
gneiss

pp. 38 to 39

(1)	urge	(2)	merge	(3)	dirge
(4)	dirt	(5)	alert	(6)	what
(7)	yacht	(8)	antique	(9)	weak
(10)	sheik	(11)	horse	(12)	of course
(13)	source	(14)	coarse	(15)	loose

(16)	excuse	(17)	juice	(18)	truce
(19)	mousse	(20)	feared	(21)	weird
(22)	sneered	(23)	tiered	(24)	adhered
(25)	rehearse	(26)	verse	(27)	worse
(28)	coerce	(29)	curse		

p. 39

1.	seen	flower	7.	reign	
2.	bier		8.	Their	fare
3.	heir	throne	9.	write	except
4.	weight	waste	10.	know	whole
5.	minor	plane	11.	threw	cellar	stairs
6.	herd	ewes			

CHAPTER 9

p. 42

infamous = disgraceful
noisome = smelly
flatulent = blown up
friable = crumbly
indifferent = unconcerned
apian = relating to bees
fulsome = sickeningly insincere

p. 43

A baseball fan might write: The batter hit a fly which the pitcher caught.

A cook might write: Catch that fly before it gets into the pitcher of pancake batter.

pp. 43 to 45

1.	impugned	imputing
2.	ingenious	ingenuous
3.	anonymous	unanimous
4.	flout	flaunt
5.	conscious	conscience
6.	incredible	incredulous
7.	indignant	indigent
8.	principle	principal
9.	adopt	adapt

10. eminent   imminent
11. allusions   illusions
12. compliment   complement
13. accept   except
14. fortuitous   fortunate
15. personnel   personal

CHAPTER 10

p. 46
ream   cream   scream

p. 47
banana

p. 50
fragment   athlete   employ
skiing   magnet   bathhouse

p. 50
understudy or overstuffed
meanwhile
underground
radioisotope

CHAPTER 11

pp. 51 to 52
slip up
desserts
sinned

p. 52
level   sexes   defied
solos   refer   rotor
civic   redder   toot
        reviver

pp. 52 to 53
1. dirty room   3. angered
2. married   4. enough

5. pirates   10. measured
6. precise   11. waitress
7. bedroom   12. spend it
8. flirting   13. mousetrap
9. remuneration

p. 53

HEAT	HOT	SICK	GOOD	HOUSE	LOSE
HEAD	HIT	SILK	FOOD	ROUSE	LOST
HELD	HIM	SILL	FOOT	ROUTE	LEST
HOLD	AIM	WILL	LOOT	ROUTS	LENT
COLD	ARM	WELL	LOST	BOUTS	LEND
	ARE		LEST	BOATS	FEND
	ACE		BEST	BRATS	FIND
	ICE			BRASS	
	ICY			GRASS	
				GLASS	
				CLASS	

p. 54

ROOM	HALL
BOOM	HELL
BOON	HELD
BORN	HEAD
BORE	READ
BARE	ROAD
BALE	ROAM
BALL	ROOM
HALL	

p. 56
The best I've come up with so far are *strength* for the consonants and *miaoued* for the vowels.

Index